WALKS AROUND HAWKSHEAD

10 WALKS UNDER 6 MILES

DALESMAN

Dalesman Publishing Company Ltd
Stable Courtyard, Broughton Hall,
Skipton, North Yorkshire BD23 3AE

First Edition 1997
Reprinted 1998

Cover: Tarn Hows by Julie Fryer

A British Library Cataloguing in Publication record is available for this book

ISBN 1 85568 118 8

Printed by Amadeus Press, Huddersfield

Contents

Introduction

These ten glorious circular walks, in the Coniston and Hawkshead area, have been devised for young families and for those who wish to dawdle on their way through the lovely countryside which lies in High Furness, Southern Lakeland, preserving its secrets from the 'madding crowds'.

The instructions and accompanying maps are detailed enough even for those people who have little experience of exploring, or who find carrying or reading a map a tiresome chore. Steep climbs and high level walks have been avoided. Points of interest have been highlighted to keep both youngsters and their parents, and older walkers too, enthralled as they go along the way.

Coniston, from where several of the walks start, is a lively village, delighting visitors as well as having a busy life of its own. The centre for most of its activities is The Institute, which houses the Ruskin Museum. John Ruskin, the 19th century writer and art critic, was a wealthy patron of the village. Brantwood, his fine home, stands on the narrow road that runs along the east side of the lake, and is open to the public. His grave can be seen in Coniston's churchyard.

Hawkshead too has a thriving tourist industry while retaining the air of a charming tiny village. It was beloved by William Wordsworth, the 19th century Lakes poet and by Beatrix Potter, the writer of children's books, the creator of Peter Rabbit and Squirrel Nutkin and others. Beatrix lived at Hill Top, Near Sawrey, two miles from Hawkshead. It too is open to the public.

All the walks pass through High Furness, perhaps the most densely wooded area in the country. Its industries of charcoal burning, iron-ore smelting and bobbin making have gone but many acres of woodland remain. Much of it is maintained by modern forestry methods and there is a place for deer, red squirrels, foxes, birds and a wide variety of wild flowers.

Walk 1

Coniston Water from Torver

Circular walk beside Coniston Water, through glorious woodland and over delightful open fell.
Length of walk: 5 miles.
Start/finish: Park in the Lake District National Park's small layby on the A5084, just below Hadwin's garage, a mile south of Torver.
Terrain: Easy walking along clear paths.

Leave the layby by a path through bracken, signposted Coniston via Lakeshore. Climb the slope for your first glimpse of the lake. Pass through a kissing gate and descend steadily to come beside a wall, over which lean some fine larch trees. Follow the clear path (Cumbria Way), watching for a glimpse of the long slim Gondola.

The steam yacht, a mixture of a Venetian gondola and an English steam yacht, was originally launched from Coniston Hall for service on Coniston Water in 1859. In 1937 her boiler was sold to power a saw mill and the hull became a houseboat. In 1963 she was stranded ashore after being washed in during a storm. In 1977 the National Trust began the long task of rebuilding her. Three years later the yacht re-entered service on Coniston and now carries 86 passengers in an opulently upholstered and heated saloon. It was on Coniston Water, in 1967, that Donald Campbell, in his boat Bluebird, tried to break the water speed record. At great speed the boat somersaulted and disappeared into the lake's very deep water. Campbell's body has never been recovered.

The path continues beside the lake and its pebbly shore. Sit on a seat on a rocky outcrop, below birch – a good place from which to enjoy the extensive view of the lovely lake. Follow the path as it climbs above the shore, passing through oaks and birch and then a large area of juniper. Step across the small stream issuing out of Moor Gill and move onto the shore to look for pieces of slag.

This is probably the site of an old bloomery. Iron ore was brought by barge from Nibthwaite at the foot of the lake to be smelted, using charcoal obtained from the coppiced woodland. It was easier to transport the ore than the enormous quantity of charcoal required for smelting.

Climb the next slope and follow the clear path to pass through a gate and then follow it as it drops down beside the lake to pass through another gate. Beyond, walk on to take the continuing waymarked path. Pass the end of a wall and go on into a grassy clearing. Fifty yards along, take the track leading left, away from the lake, signposted Torver.

Stride the good path, ignoring any side turns, through more woodland. Go through a gate and saunter on, with Coniston Old Man ahead. Pass through the next gate to walk a walled track. Climb the stile and continue along another wide track to pass some lofty beeches on your left. Stroll on to cross a narrow lane and take the stile opposite. Beyond follow the path as it meanders a little, with Torver church away to your left, to a ladderstile to the trackbed of the old Furness railway.

In 1859 Coniston village was linked by rail to Foxfield. This enabled large quantities of slate quarried in the fells to be carried away for processing. In 1958 this delightful nine-mile line, which also carried goods, tourists, school children and many passengers, passing through glorious countryside, was closed. Go up the opposite side of the track and walk ahead to pass through a gap in the fence and on to a kissing gate to the A593. Turn left, cross the bridge over Torver Beck and take the narrow lane on your right. After 75 yards, climb the sturdy stone-stepped stile on the left. Walk ahead on a walled grassy track. Climb the next stile. Fifty yards along go through the easy-to-miss gap stile on the left and then straight ahead across the pasture to another stile beneath a tall ash. Pass through a gap ahead and walk on with the wall to your left. Follow it to a step-stile beside the churchyard and opposite Church House Inn.

Walk right to pass the Wilson Arms and take the quiet lane that runs parallel with (to the right of) the busy A-road. Take the signposted gate on the left, beyond the last cottage. Stride ahead to a gate to the busy road. Cross to take the stile opposite. Walk ahead to cross a footbridge and a stile. Walk on to the right corner of the pasture to take a gate onto a narrow lane. Bear left and immediately walk right along another narrow lane. Where it swings sharp right, go through the well waymarked gate on the left. Continue on the clear way until you reach Torver Mill (a three-storeyed dwelling) on your left.

For several centuries there was a corn and fulling mill (or walk-mill) at Torver. In fulling, the woollen cloth was walked upon or pounded by hand and then stretched out on sunny banks to dry, held in place by pegs.

Do not cross the bridge but turn right to walk another walled track. Pass through the gate onto the common and go ahead along the track following the overhead power lines. Stroll on with the attractive disused reservoir to your right.

When the path comes to a small dam, on your right, and before you cross the small beck issuing from the reservoir, turn left and descend for 150 yards beside the tree-lined gill now on your right. Turn left and dawdle along the good track that goes downhill, steadily, through the lovely Mere Gill to a footbridge over the Torver Beck. Beyond follow the path up the slope. Cross the road to rejoin your car in the layby opposite.

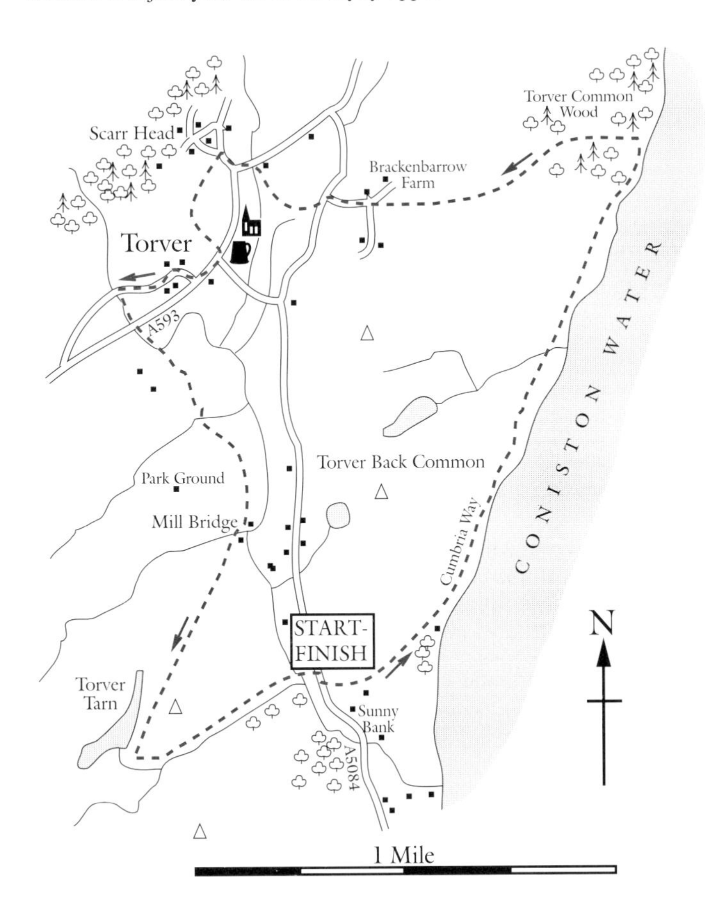

Walk 2

Coppermines Valley

Circular walk from Coniston village through the Coppermines Valley and over open fell below the Old Man of Coniston.
Length of walk: 4 miles.
Start/finish: Pay-and-display car park on the site of the old railway station. To reach this take the turn in the middle of the village, almost opposite the petrol station, and follow the signs uphill. There is also parking at the top of the hill, by the first stile, but this would involve doing the hill climb at the end of the walk.
Terrain: Generally easy walking. A steady climb until above The Bell.

The Old Man of Coniston broods overhead throughout this walk. Its summit rears proudly skywards in spite of great chunks of its lovely green slate having been gouged from its sides and its mass bored through with copper miners' tunnels. Climb the steps out of the end of the car park. Cross the narrow road and go on into deciduous woodland, walking over exposed slate. Follow the path as it swings right to join the road, with a glorious view of the hills ahead. Go on up the steep narrow road, pausing frequently to enjoy the vista, right, into the Yewdale Valley. To your left a small stream chuckles on its way to Coniston Water as it passes through birch and ash. Where the lane swings sharp left and there is a large layby, climb the stile on the right, signposted Miners Bridge.

Walk ahead with the wall to your right and continue to the gate just before the Scrow Beck. Look for the piece of slate used as part of the gate's hinge. Once through the gate, turn left and cross the beck on a footbridge. The word scrow is used on farms in the area to mean a mess, but the name hardly seems appropriate here because where the beck tumbles over its rocky bed there is only a quiet delectable hollow in the hills.

Bear right to continue on a pleasing path, still with the wall to your right. Enjoy the view of the lake, with Grizedale Forest beyond. Descend the path to come to the side of Church Beck, which you cross on Miners Bridge. Turn left to walk into the Coppermines Valley. In the 16th century Daniel Hochstetter, a German mining engineer, surveyed the Old Man for minerals and found rich lodes of copper on its eastern face. German miners, already busy in Keswick, came to Coniston to exploit the ore, which was sent back by packhorse to the smelters at Keswick.

The wide track, beside the unfenced gorge of Church Beck, leads into the valley bottom. Walk on along the track to see the great heaps of spoil. As you go think of the miners who, every morning, with candles stuck in their hats, clambered down shaky ladders to wrest the ore from galleries below sea-level. Some of the spoil came from slate quarrying. Vast quantities of slate were being removed from the Old Man's slopes in the 18th century. It was carried by packhorse to the lakeshore and from there by barge to Greenodd to be shipped to other parts of the country. As you walk, listen for blasting from today's quarrying just below the summit of the Old Man.

The several buildings in the valley were all part of these two industries. The row of cottages, now used by holiday makers, was once named Irish Row after the Irishmen who came in great numbers to work in the valley. The single-storeyed white building is now a youth hostel. To continue , return to the Miners Bridge and, just before you cross, walk a few more steps to see Church Beck's spectacular waterfall. Beyond the bridge turn right to walk the clear track, from where you have another good view of the Coppermines Valley. Look high up on the slopes beyond Irish Row to see the remains of winding gear used by the miners. Pass through the wall and go on up the track, now almost under the shadow of the Old Man. Between you and the summit is the quarry from where the blasting was taking place.

One short grassy scramble brings you to a reinforced track. Here turn left and stride the grand track with the aptly named hill, The Bell, to your left and the streams that form Scrow Beck to your right. As you go look left across the hills to see the Howgills and to the right of these the flat top of Ingleborough in Yorkshire is visible in the far distance. To the immediate left, tucked into a corner between walls, stands the ruin of an old cottage. Stride on to come to a cross of tracks and roads and a three-armed signpost. Ignore the intersecting way and go on ahead along a bridleway. Follow the hoof prints of the horses and stroll on beside the wall on your left.

After 500 yards, and just before the fourth wall going off left (you'll have to keep looking over the wall on your left), pass through a gate. Continue ahead along a path as the horses do. Descend steadily to a hollow through which a small beck dances. Step across, using a large grassy tuft mid-stream and go on down the clear walled track, with the stream hurrying beside you on your left. From here you have an excellent view of the lake.

Just before the track swings right into a short walled track, take the gate on the left onto a track, with the stream beside you on the left. Pass through the next gate and continue down the track to take a kissing gate to join the permissive footpath along the disused railway track, where you turn left. Continue on the delightful tree-lined track of the old Furness railway, pass under a high-arched bridge and stroll on to the site of the railway station to rejoin your car.

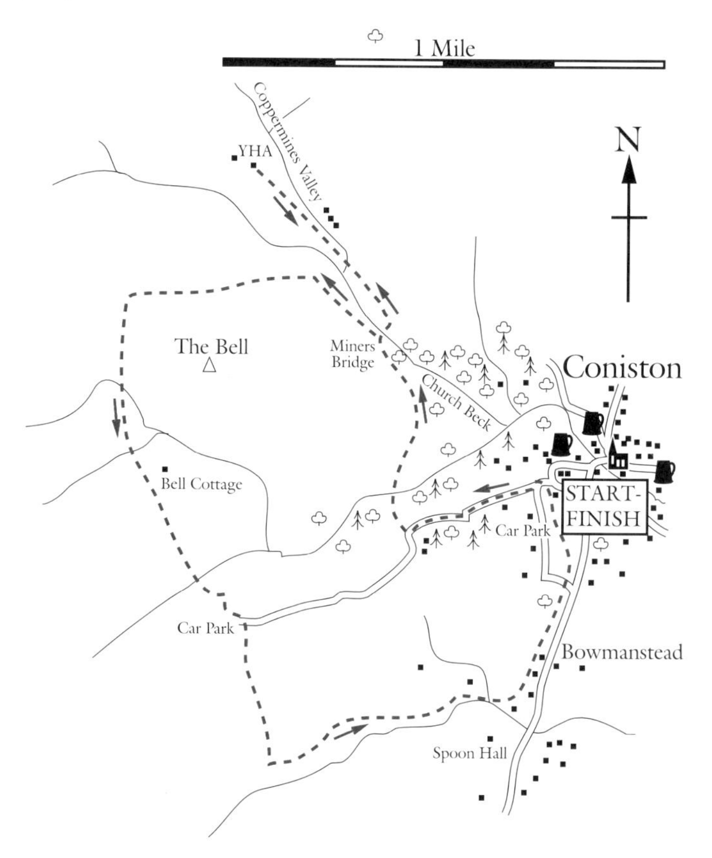

Walk 3

Coniston to Tarn Hows

A circular walk from Coniston village over glorious undulating pastures and through pleasing deciduous woodland via Tarn Hows.
Length of walk: 5 miles (6 if you walk round Tarn Hows).
Start/finish: Pay and display car park in centre of Coniston, beside the Information Centre.
Terrain: Easy walking generally. The descent by the waterfalls is an exciting, but safe, scramble.

Leave the car park, cross Ruskin Avenue and walk on along Tilberthwaite Avenue, with shops to your left. Just before Yewdale Bridge, turn left and walk the lane with the Yewdale Beck to your right. Opposite the primary school, take the signposted footpath to cross Shepherd Bridge. A stepped stile on the left, at the end of the bridge, gives access to the side of the stream and the path then passes through a sturdy gate.

Beyond, follow the clear path over a hay meadow, where you are asked to stay on the path and keep all dogs on leads. Go on below oaks and then climb gently beside a drystone wall on the left. To the right stands a folly-like structure, which was used for housing Coniston foxhounds at the turn of the century. Pass through the kissing gate and another. Pause here for a good view of Coniston Water. Climb the stile, set in a wire fence, into a small enclosure of ancient yews and then pass through the kissing gate into mixed woodland.

Emerge from the trees by a stile to continue ahead along a terrace-like path with spectacular views of the Lakeland mountains. Follow the path as it goes on, parallel with woodland to your right. Look for the waymark on the oak tree, the path keeping to the left of it. Go through the gate ahead and on over the undulating pasture to a stile to the left of a gate onto a cart track. Turn left and stride on the delectable way. On reaching the footbridge over the Yewdale Beck, do not cross but take the stile on the right.

The path keeps close beside a newly set hedge on your left. Climb the stile that brings you to the side of the beck and then follow the path as it moves away from the stream and ascends through the glorious woodland.

In a small clearing, ignore the stile in the deer fence and walk on up with the deer netting to your right – watching for deer as you go. Join a track and stroll on. Enjoy more spectacular views and then pass through two gates to come to the signpost in front of the charming Tarn Hows Cottage. Turn right in the direction of Tarn Hows and pass through the next gate. Follow the access road as it curves left.

Just before the access road joins a narrow road, turn left to descend a walled bridleway. After 400 yards, and when you can just glimpse the Coniston to Ambleside road through the trees, take the unsignposted gate on your right. Walk ahead, ignoring the tractor route that bears off left. The grassy way proceeds between the remnants of two old walls. Stride on to pass to the left of a ruined farmhouse and follow the track as it takes a sharp left turn on its zig-zagging way up the slope.

Climb the grand grassy way, with a derelict wall below to your left. Head towards woodland and follow the track as it bears right beside it. Take your time on this short steep way and watch for a gate on your left into woodland. Dawdle on and once over the brow of the slope you have your first view of Tarn Hows. This picturesque stretch of water, in its sylvan setting, was once three tarns. James Marshall, who lived at nearby Monk Coniston Hall, merged them into one to provide water power for his saw mills in the valley.

Here you need to make a decision. If you wish to walk the good paths around the tarn it will take you an hour to traverse the one-and-a-half miles. If, after a pause and perhaps your picnic, you decide to forgo a walk round the tarn, cross the outflow stream and small dam to your left, and take the rough path that descends steadily through the deciduous woodland of Tom Gill, keeping close to the tumbling stream on your left.

Parts of the path have been pitched to make walking easier, but watch out for exposed tree roots just waiting to trip you. Go through a kissing gate and, after dropping down through the oak trees, pause to look back at the plummeting triple waterfall. Stay with the beck until you reach the busy road, seen earlier.

Cross and walk left, with care, for 75 yards. Turn right into the signposted access track for Yew Tree farm. The farm has a round chimney. Such chimneys were easier to build with the stone available and it was believed there were no corners for the devil to hide in. From here you can see the farm's famous spinning gallery. It might have been used occasionally for spinning, but in reality it provided ready access to other rooms upstairs and was a useful storage area.

Go on the track as it swings right and then bears left, keeping beside the wall on your left. Pass through a kissing gate onto the fell and bear left to dawdle along the delightful permissive gated way. This keeps generally beside the wall on your left and brings you to a narrow lane. Cross Shepherd's Bridge (a second bridge on this walk carrying the same name) and turn left to rejoin the busy road. Turn right and walk on. Ignore the right turn and after 50 yards take the gate on your right into more pleasing oak woodland.

Follow the path through the trees to climb a ladderstile. Strike right to climb another and walk on a short distance. Pause here to look over the wall to see a fine limekiln which made use of the limestone that outcrops here and is part of the narrow band that runs from Shap to the head of the Duddon estuary. Stride on to the footbridge over White Gill. After heavy rain the beck descends in foaming cascades, known as White Lady waterfall, over the slopes of Yewdale Crag. Go on through the trees to rejoin the road at Far End. Turn right and then take the right turn off the A-road. Follow the narrow road as it swings left and rejoins the main road. Turn right to walk into the centre of Coniston. Just before the bridge over Church Beck, turn left to return to the car park.

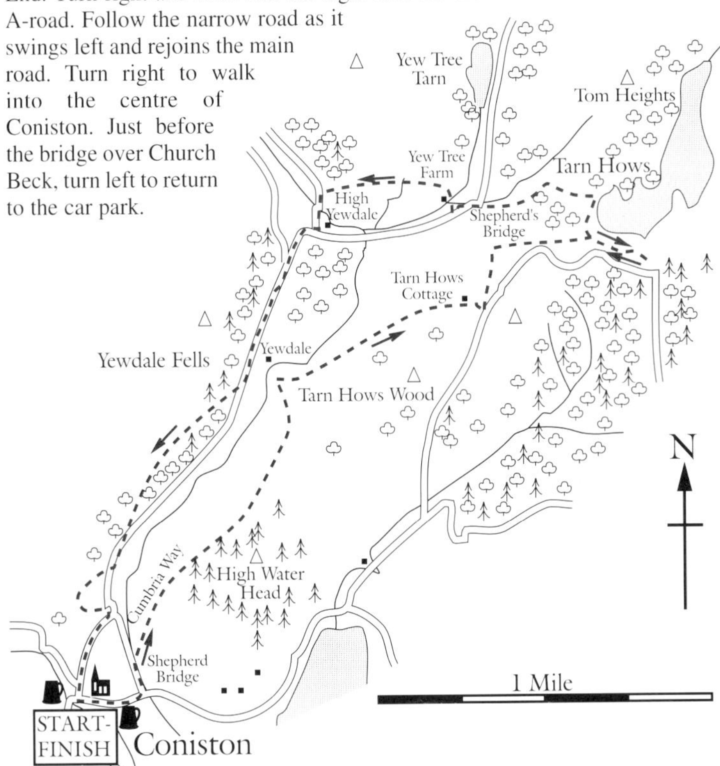

Walk 4

Yewdale Valley

Circular walk from the head of Coniston Water over the quiet pastures of Yewdale, surrounded by high fells.
Length of walk: 4 miles.
Start/finish: The National Trust's pay-and-display Monk Coniston car park off the Nibthwaite road at the head of Coniston Water.
Terrain: Easy walking except for one short climb up a grassy pasture.

From the car park join the pebbly beach and walk keeping the lake on your left. The water is shallow enough for paddling and there are several seats from which you can view the length of the lake. Continue on the shingle to a fence barring your way, where you move right to join the road. Cross to pass through a gate and turn right. Stride on the wide footpath to a gate to the road. Pause here to see a spinning gallery (see walk 3). Join the road and, after ten steps, turn left into a wide track to pass through the National Trust wood yard.

Stroll on to pass the 16th century Boon Crag farm on your right. Look here for the typical Lakeland sheep called Herdwicks. They are very hardy and can survive bitter winters. The lambs are born almost black and get lighter in colour as they grow. Walk on along the walled and hedged track, ignoring all side turns, to cross the stone bridge over the Yewdale Beck. Follow the track as it swings right in front of a barn and then pass in front of Low Yewdale Farm, which replaced the older farm that you pass next.Go through the gate and carry on with a fine view of the Yewdale Fells and, ahead, the wild face of Raven Crag. Go through three more gates and then turn left and walk on.

Before you pass through the gate to the road, look across to see High Yewdale Farm. To the left of the one lived in today is a 17th century farmhouse. Cross the road, turn left and walk 75 yards to turn right into a narrow lane, signposted Hodge Close. Just before you cross Shepherd's Bridge, look for the ford where some of the family might wish to cross if the beck is low enough. Once over the bridge pass through the kissing gate on your right, signposted Skelwith Bridge. Go through the next two gates. Press on to take the kissing gate on the right. Walk the track beyond and follow it as it swings right, from where you can see the picturesque farmhouse and its spinning gallery (walk 3).

Cross the A-road with care, walk right for a few steps and take the signposted gate on your left. Ahead is a low post with an arrow directing you straight up the pathless slope to the top corner of a walled wood. Pause frequently as you climb to enjoy the unfolding views. At the corner of the wood, bear right through a gate and then turn left. Go on uphill beside the fence, and then a wall, on your left. Pass through the gateless gap in the top left corner, turn right and continue with the wall of Tarn Hows Cottage to your right. Follow the wall round to pass through a gate on the right, in front of the pretty cottage. Turn left to walk the track, signposted Coniston.

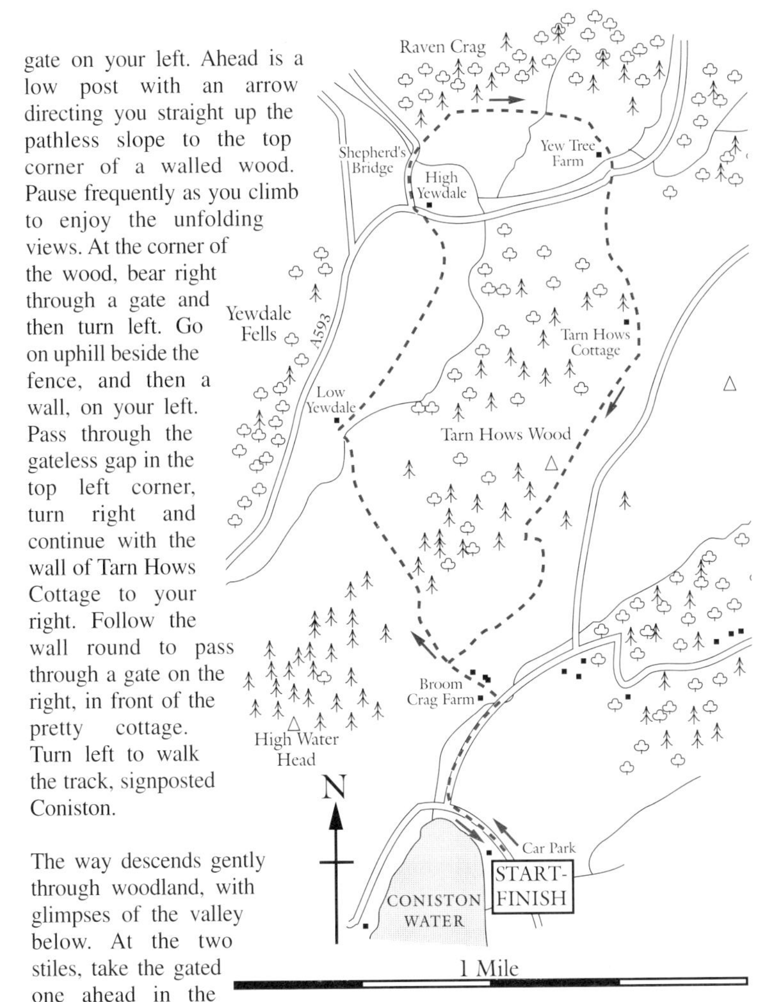

The way descends gently through woodland, with glimpses of the valley below. At the two stiles, take the gated one ahead in the wire fence, which is tall enough to keep deer out of the plantation of young trees. Continue down the path to leave by a similar stile. Beyond, the ways divide and you need to take the wide grassy track on the left. This winds gently downhill to the track taken on your outward route. Turn left and continue to the road, beyond Boon Crag Farm. Turn right, pass through the gate on the right to walk the track towards the head of the lake. Cross the road and walk across the beach to return to the car park.

Walk 5

Tilberthwaite Gill

Circular walk from Tilberthwaite Gill along good tracks, through deciduous woodland, across open fell and over an unusual bridge.
Length of walk: 4 miles.
Start/finish: Two parking areas on either side of Yewdale Beck, where it issues from Tilberthwaite Gill. The turning for the gill leaves the A593, 1½ miles north of Coniston, or four-and-a-half miles south of Ambleside. It is the turning referred to towards the end of walk 4.
Terrain – Easy walking through glorious countryside.

As you leave the parking area to continue along the narrow road, look left to see a Lakeland cottage with a fine spinning gallery (walk 3). Go through the kissing gate at the road end and cross the yard of the farm, diagonally left, to pass through a gate onto a steadily climbing track. The way goes on through oak and birch woodland, where you might glimpse a red squirrel, and then crosses open fell, with dramatic mountain slopes to your left.

Beyond the next gate walk on, with a glorious view, away to the left, of the Langdale Pikes. Soon you can look down on Little Langdale Tarn. Pause regularly to enjoy the walled pastures and white-washed farmhouses of Little Langdale, nestling in a hollow almost surrounded by mountains. Go through a kissing gate and descend to a Y-junction of tracks. Pause again to enjoy the grand vista. Turn right and stroll on, with the pretty tarn to your left, the still water pleasingly reflecting the steep slopes of Lingmoor. Go through a gate with an old yew tree beside it. Pass High Hallgarth, a cottage with a typical Lakeland porch. The way continues below a huge hill of spoil from earlier quarrying, the higgledy-piggledy slate softened with lichen, moss and young birch. Go on down the slope and follow the track right to pass another picturesque cottage.

Carry on along the track and take the gate in the wall on your left. Cross the pasture, climb the step-stile and walk across Slater Bridge over the River Brathay, where it flows out of the tarn. One half of the bridge makes use of great slabs of slate and the other half is a delightful arch.

This ancient bridge, of the packhorse type, was once the boundary between

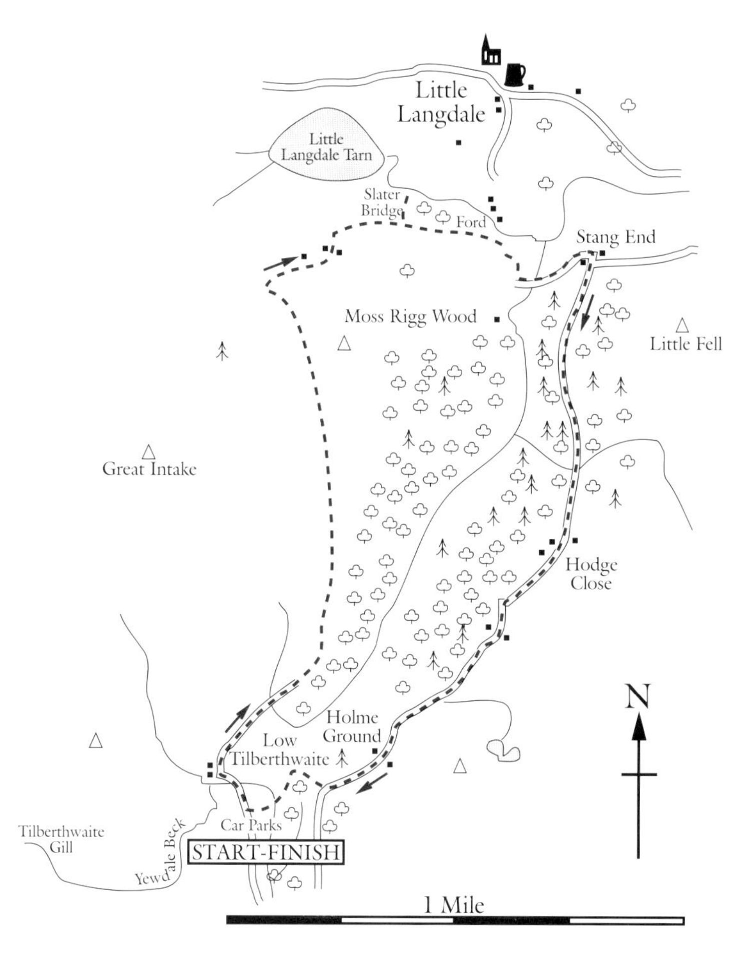

Westmorland and Lancashire. In 1941 it was in a bad state of repair; children could not step over a hole in the middle and one passer-by dropped her packages into the water through the hole. Beatrix Potter, the writer of children's books and a great benefactor, of the Lake District, offered to let the local council have timber from her woodland to repair it. Eventually it was repaired. An outcrop of rock nearby is just the place for a picnic and a photo-stop.

Return over the bridge and pasture to rejoin the track, and go on (left) along the gated track until you reach a ford and bridge over the river. Do not cross but follow the track right and where, almost immediately, it branches, take the left fork, signposted Skelwith Bridge. The good track edges left through trees, crosses a stone bridge and then ascends through open pastures. As you approach Stang End farmhouse on your left, look right to see another spinning gallery on a barn on the right, with bee-boles in the wall below.

Bee-boles are rectangular recesses set deep in a drystone wall. At the end of the summer hives of bees were brought down from the fells. Hives, or skeps, were made of heather or straw, and these were placed in the alcoves to protect the bees from the winter weather.

Take the right turn opposite Stang End, signposted Hodge Close. Climb the gated track, with deciduous woodland to the left and a wall to your right. Continue until you reach a gate on your right, which you take into extensive oak woodland. Pass a house and a cottage, and then more cottages. At this point any young children must be kept under tight control as the track continues fairly close to an enormous quarry. At a safe distance it is fun to watch the abseilers descend the sheer sides. Divers frequent the deep ultramarine-coloured pool in the quarry bottom.

Go on along the metalled way to pass Holme Ground cottages, with Holme Fell away to the left. Saunter on past two fine stone houses. Ignore the signposted path to the farm and take the next footpath on the right into woodland. Keep on the main path and just before a gate, take the narrow path up through trees, signposted 'To the car park'. The path then drops down to a gate to the side of the Yewdale Beck. Turn right and walk beside the wall on the right to a gap stile to the road and the parking area.

Walk 6

Latterbarrow

Circular walk from Hawkshead to the glorious top of Latterbarrow.
Length of walk: 4 miles.
Start/finish: Hawkshead's pay-and-display car park, situated on the road that by-passes the village on its east side.
Terrain: Easy walking.

This walk passes through quiet pastures around the charming village of Hawkshead, through Claife Heights woods on easy tracks, culminating with a short climb to Latterbarrow for one of Lakeland's great views.

Turn right (north east) out of the car park and then walk left (north west) for 200 yards. Cross the road and take the signposted track that curves right, and then left, to pass Black Beck Lodge and Cottage, both bequeathed to the National Trust by Beatrix Potter. Cross the footbridge over Black Beck and bear left and then right over a pasture to a waymarked kissing gate. Continue on the clear track over the next pasture to pass through another kissing gate.

Beyond, turn right and stroll on in the direction of Colthouse. A kissing gate gives access to a reinforced track, which you cross to pass through another gate. Climb the steepish slope and follow the path where it swings slightly right to an easy-to-miss waymarked stile in the wall, which is now to your left. Once through the stone-stepped stile, go ahead, bearing a little left to pass through a gap in the wall. Follow the waymarks, walking beside a fence on the right and the wall of a dwelling on your left. Turn left to pass between it and another dwelling to climb a stile to join a narrow road. Go right and walk to a T-junction. Turn left and in a few yards take the signposted gated track on the right.

The clear track goes on and on, steadily upward, and comes beside a small tarn. Look out as you go for red squirrels and maybe the bright red flash of a fox, hurrying through the woodland undergrowth. Pass through a gate, beyond which is a three-armed signpost. Here turn left, following the way for Latterbarrow. From now on the route through the forest is waymarked with white -topped posts. These direct you along a track that gradually bears left to come to the bottom of some reinforced steps that climb steeply upward. At the top, follow the path right, with a wall to your right. Press on over a wet area and then the path climbs a little, more light enters the forest and you come to a stile with an interesting dog gate. Beyond you are on open fell. Take the path climbing up through the bracken to stand by the fine cairn on the top of the small hill. Pause here to enjoy the magnificent view; perhaps this is the place you will choose for your picnic.

Before you leave, walk right to look down on Windermere. Leave the cairn by one of the grassy swathes, through the bracken, that descend left towards a stream and a wall (the wall beside which you would walk if you did not wish to visit the cairn). Follow the good track, down and down, to the road, where you turn left. In a few yards, turn right to walk for 600 yards along very quiet Loanthwaite Lane. Escape from the road by a second footpath on the left, signposted 'Hawkshead.' Follow the well waymarked route as it swings right and then left to a kissing gate. Go through the next gate and walk for a few yards along a narrow track to take another gate on the right. Carry on heading towards the village until you reach the footbridge crossed at the outset of the walk. Continue, to rejoin your car.

Leave time to explore the lovely village with its narrow streets, tiny alleys, small squares and pretty dwellings. It also has some good shops and a Beatrix Potter Gallery which is housed in the Bump or Bend Cottage, where William Heelis, Beatrix Potter's solicitor husband, had his office. It formed part of the Heelis bequest to the National Trust.

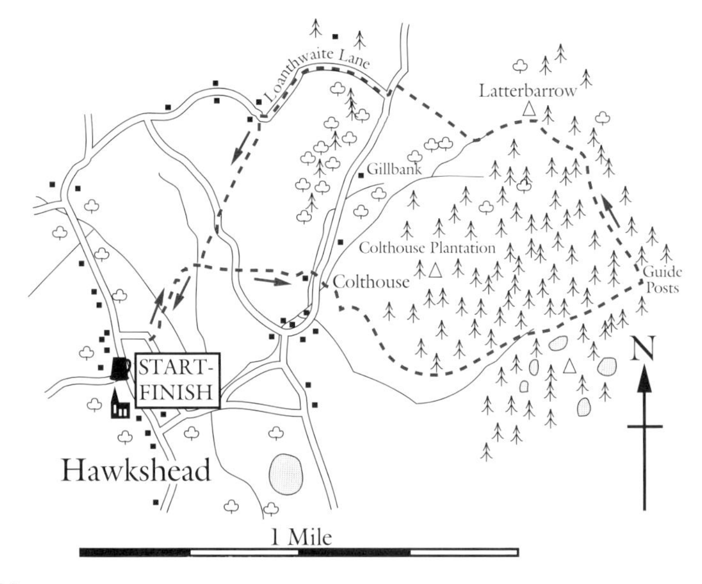

Walk 7

Hawkshead Moor

Circular walk from Hawkshead via Hawkshead Moor.
Length of walk: 4 miles.
Start/finish: Hawkshead car park on east side of village.
Terrain: Easy walking all the way.

Glimpses of Esthwaite Water and Windermere, fine rolling pastures and grand deciduous woodland, all conspire to make this a most attractive walk. Turn left out of the car park and walk towards the parish church of St Michael and All Angels. Just before you reach the church you pass the Grammar School. It was given this name because its pupils were taught Latin grammar. It was founded by Archbishop Sandys in 1585 and its most famous pupil was William Wordsworth, who carved his name on one of the desks.

Beyond, on its hillock stands Hawkshead's fine church. Go inside and look for the Sandys Chapel built by the archbishop, the list of churchwardens for 1711 and the painted murals on the walls. These were done by James Addison in 1680. Later they were covered with whitewash and were revealed in 1875 when the walls were cleaned. Continue on beyond the church to pass through a gate. Once through the next gate, walk left following the signpost in the direction of Roger Ground. Carry on along the delightful well waymarked path to walk a fenced and hedged way. Look for the notched Brathay flags used extensively for fencing.

At the road, turn right and stroll uphill for 50 yards to take the track on your left, signposted Howe Farm, passing through the hamlet of Roger Ground. At the end of the track, bear right, to go through a white metal gate to saunter on, with How Beck to your left. As you proceed, look left for your first sighting of Esthwaite Water, where Wordsworth liked to walk before school. Take the gate on your left just before the farm and swing right to a gate onto the farm's access track, where you turn left to walk to the road.

Go right, with care, for 200 yards. From the road you can see more of the flagged fencing. Turn right into a wide signposted track. Keep left of the dwellings at Eldergill and follow the clear way through deciduous woodland, with the dancing beck to your right. Emerge from the trees by a stile, cross a small ford and follow the waymarked path as it swings left and

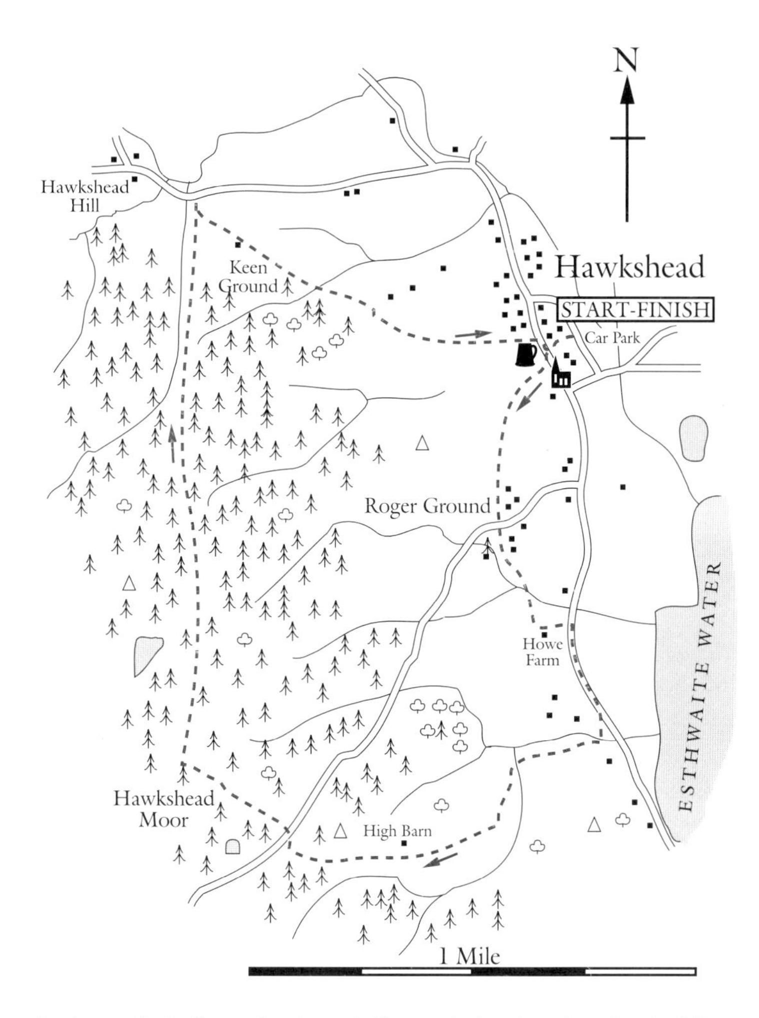

begins to climb. Go on the clear winding track. At a junction of paths follow the waymark right to pass through bracken. Pause as you go to enjoy the magnificent views and the wonderful quiet, and then go on to the stile. Beyond turn right and keep beside the wall on your right. Follow the path to a waymark at the top of the slope. Proceed to the next waymark and then to a stile in front of High Barn, passing between the dwelling and its barn. Join the reinforced track and at the four-armed signpost go ahead, following the sign for Grizedale, to reach a road.

Turn right and in a few yards turn left into the woodland of Moor Top, part of Grizedale Forest Park. At the Y-junction take the right branch, marked with a red banded trail post. On reaching a junction of two forest roads and a reinforced track, take the latter – the middle one – and climb uphill through the delightful mixed young woodland. When you reach a forest road, turn right and almost immediately turn right again to walk a waymarked track.

Stroll the pleasing way. Look for a small tarn on your left, set in a wooded hollow. At a junction of several tracks, ignore the right and left and walk ahead, watching out for your first view of the Langdale Pikes. At the T-junction, cross the forest road to take a narrow path dropping downhill. It is waymarked with a yellow arrow. Leave the forest by a kissing gate and go ahead, keeping close to the beck on your left. Cross an access track to a farm, away to your right, to go through a gate. Go on to join the road. Turn right and immediately take a gate on your right into a pasture.

Climb the clear path up the slope to cross the main access track to the farm and go on along the wide track. Pass through a gate into a copse. Descend the steps to cross a tiny stream. Walk on along a path of slate to cross another beck on a concrete tractor bridge. Bear left to walk beside the hurrying water to a kissing gate. Press on along the wide way over the lovely pastures to pass through two more kissing gates. Descend to a gate to a narrow lane, where you turn left.

This narrow lane quickly takes you into Hawkshead, passing tiny cottages, archways and cobbled squares, and to Anne Tyson's cottage. William Wordsworth lodged with Anne while a scholar at the Grammar School from 1779 until 1787. On the left of the cottage and up some steps is the chapel where William occasionally worshipped.

Continue on, to explore more of the village. Look for the tiny cottage whose front is hung with slates, the building whose corner is shaped to allow carts to pass, Pillar House with an outside staircase and the Town Hall.

Walk 8

Grizedale Forest Park

Circular walk through Grizedale Forest Park.
Length of walk: 5 miles.
Start/finish: Pay-and-display car park at Grizedale Visitor Centre. This lies 2 miles south of Hawkshead.
Terrain: Generally easy gradients. Some tracks rough.

Grizedale Forest Park is managed by Forest Enterprise, part of the Forestry Commission. The charcoal burners' hearths, once so busy, have long since gone cold and the bloomeries fallen silent, but the forest still provides for the needs of industry. Every day five lorries leave laden with timber. It has an interesting Visitor Centre and many miles of paths and tracks which include ten waymarked trails. This walk makes use of part of the red banded trail and uses two old rights of way that existed before the forest was developed.

From the Visitor Centre follow the signpost arm with the red footprint. This directs you past picnic tables on the right. Just before the adventure playground, turn left to pass through a green painted door in a high wall. Turn right and follow the trail marker posts banded with red. Walk the metalled lane. Pass Home Farm and follow the curving way. Take the waymarked track on the left, signposted Coniston Water. Climb the rough path over exposed rock. At the forest road, walk right. Look for the narrow track leading off uphill on the left, with a red banded post at the start. This is the way the walk continues.

As you pass an area where the trees have been felled pause to look at the contours of the forest floor. This is what the fellside looked like before the trees were planted, difficult to visualise when in the depths of a thriving plantation. Pause again by two old gate stoops to look down on the pleasing pastures of the dale. Beyond, the track levels and the way is a delight to walk. Cross a small stream and enjoy the lush ferns and grasses that clothe its banks. Walk on. The red route now turns left, but this walk continues ahead to a T-junction of wide forest roads. Note this point for your return. Turn right and in a few steps, where the track divides, take the left branch. Stride on with, ahead, the first of many magnificent views of the Old Man of Coniston and of Wetherlam. After a gentle descent, take a clear track on the left.

On reaching a remnant of drystone wall and an iron fence the path divides again. Here take the left branch, keeping left of the 'Do not start a fire' sign. Pause often on this rough path to enjoy the pleasing views ahead. Emerge from the mixed woodland by a gate and continue descending through rolling pastures, with glimpses of Coniston Water to your left. Cross Black Beck on a tractor bridge and follow the track as it swings right to pass through a gate. Go on down and down and at the next signpost follow the track round left to a gate. Beyond, walk on to join the road.

Turn left and go carefully, for 150 yards to take the signposted bridleway on the left. Climb the delightful track to recross Black Beck, now nearer its destination in the lake, by another tractor bridge. Continue through woodland, looking for evidence of coppicing. Trees which have six or seven trunks coming straight out of the soil, instead of the usual one, have been coppiced in years gone by. The poles were harvested every 18 to 23 years and used for charcoal to smelt iron ore.

Pass through a gate and stride the good track through woodland. Then the trees are left behind and you carry on beside a small barn. Sit on a nearby boulder and enjoy Coniston Water below, where you might see the Gondola steaming away on its tour of the lake. Go on to cross a small stream and pass through a gate. Press on along the good track, with a conifer plantation to your left. Pass through the next gate to come to a raised area overlooking an old farmhouse, known as Lawson Park, the experimental station in the book 'Plague Dogs' by Richard Adams. Here turn left into more dense conifers, passing between two gate-posts. (Ignore the sharp left turn, which ends abruptly.) The way now climbs steadily and becomes wider. It continues through even denser conifers, where the temperature drops rapidly. Eventually the path levels and joins a forest road, where you turn left.

Stride on to the T-junction noted on your outward way. Turn right. Fifty yards on take the red banded trail that goes off right – the one you abandoned on

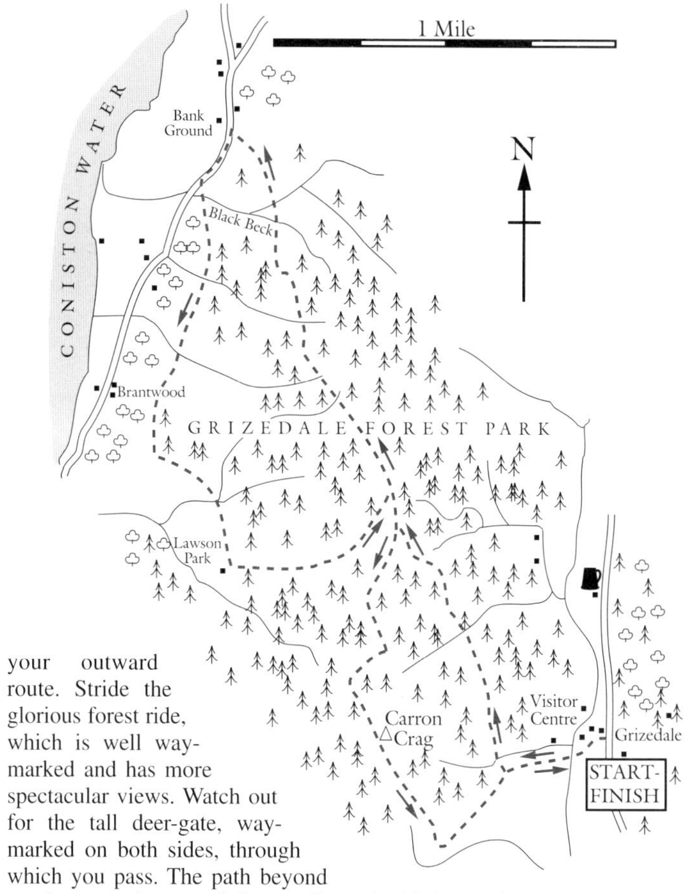

your outward route. Stride the glorious forest ride, which is well way-marked and has more spectacular views. Watch out for the tall deer-gate, way-marked on both sides, through which you pass. The path beyond continues to the top of Carron Crag, the highest point in the Forest Park (1,025 feet). Scramble to the top for breath-taking views of the Lakeland Fells, the Howgills and the waters of Morecambe Bay.

Descend from the crag and follow the marker posts to another deer gate. Beyond, turn right and, after a few yards, at a cross of tracks, bear sharp left. Descend the lovely way to a forest road, Cross and descend the rough track taken at the outset of your walk. At the road bear right and walk past the Home Farm. Look for the green door in the wall on the left to return to the Visitor Centre.

Walk 9

Force Falls

A circular walk through Grizedale Forest Park from Blind Lane.
Length of walk: 5 miles.
Start/finish: Blind Lane car park, north-east of Force Mills. Take the B-road south from Grizedale Visitor Centre towards Satterthwaite. Continue to Force Mills and turn left. The car park is on the left.
Terrain: A glorious walk on forest roads, tracks. Some steepish paths.

As much of this walk is in the forest, choose a good day when the sun slants through the glorious woodland. After rain Force Falls are stupendous but the stones and tree roots of the paths through the forest can be slippery. From each high point on the walk the views are spectacular. Leave enough time to visit the church at Satterthwaite, to browse around the potash pit and ponder on the meanings of the stone and wood sculptures positioned throughout this walk.

As with Walk 7, parts of this route lie along banded trails and the remainder – very little – on rights of way. Leave the car park by the top left corner, arrowed Force Falls and with a white and green banded trail marker post. Climb the narrow path through birch woodland. Join the track, along which you continue for a very short distance before dropping down again following the marker posts. At a junction of paths, turn left and go on down the slope, with the noise of the falls blotting out all other sounds.

Cross the narrow road with care and turn left. After 20 yards, pass through an iron kissing gate on the right for the best view of the falls. The falls are magnificent in spate and delightful to idle beside when the water level is low. Close by is Force Forge, where a 17th century smithy used the energy of the beck and the abundant charcoal to produce iron. Return to the road and turn left. Re-join the waymarked trail that enters the trees, on the left, and continue upstream, on the well maintained, delightful path, until you reach the road, which you cross.

Walk ahead along the farm track to take a footpath on the right. Climb up through deciduous woodland to an unusual shelter from where you can sit and enjoy a grand view across the valley and towards the Lakeland mountains. Leave by the continuing waymarked path, which soon becomes a forest road. Go on for 250 yards and then, just before a plantation of regimented conifers,

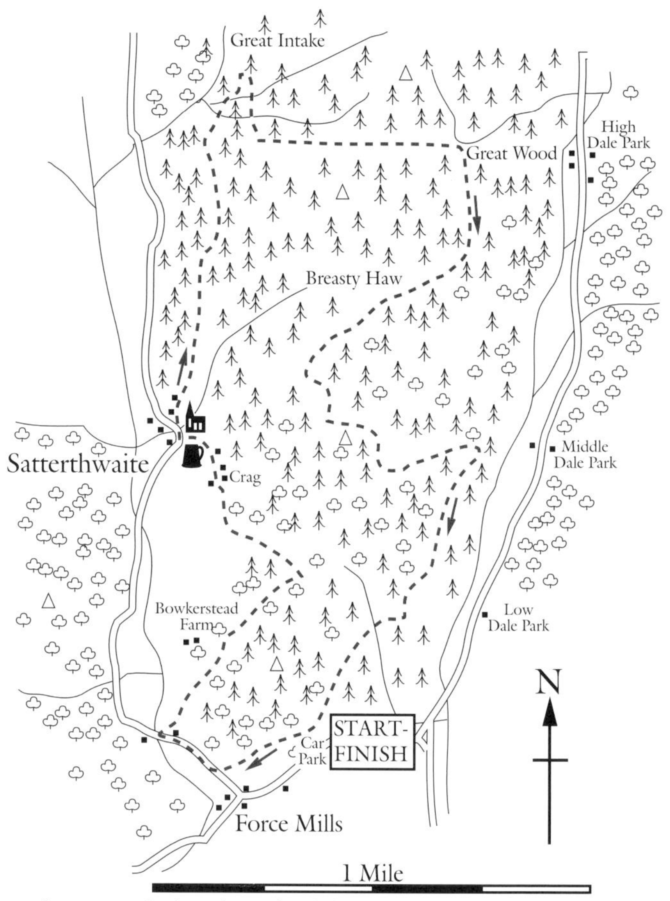

leave the waymarked road, turning left onto an indistinct unmarked right of way. This rapidly becomes a clear wide way that descends pleasingly through deciduous woodland, and then beside pastures, to the village of Satterthwaite (thwaite, Norse for a clearing in a forest). Visit the parish church of All Saints, where younger members of the family will enjoy looking at the illustrated texts that tell, in a simple way, the history of the valley.

Turn right beyond the church and take the first right turn. Climb the slope and turn right again to continue along a narrow lane until you reach the forest entrance, opposite a cottage. Just inside the gate, turn left to follow the blue banded trail posts. The path goes on along the same contour. Climb a stone-stepped stile and beyond follow the path to join another, marked with blue and red banded posts. Just beyond this point you come to the restored potash pit on your left. Bracken rich in potash, and twigs left over from harvesting coppice wood, were burnt in potash pits. The pits were built on sloping ground so that they could be fed easily from the top and the ash raked out from below. The ash was added to mutton fat to make soap to wash cloth.

Go on to join a forest road, where you turn right, remaining on the red and blue trail. Notice the wood sculptures set back in the trees. Carry on along the road and watch out for the waymarked sharp left turn that climbs steadily left, through conifers to cross a forest track. Press on the red and blue trail for a short distance and at a cross of tracks go on along the blue banded (no red bands) path. This leads steadily upwards to another glorious viewpoint and a sculpture. Descend the narrow path and look left for another very large sculpture – certainly a teaser. At the forest road, turn right. Ignore all footpaths and the blue route, as they leave the forest road. Stride on following the green banded trail posts. Watch out for the idyllic tarn to the left of the road, with two more fascinating sculptures set in the water and on a small island.

At the Y-junction go on the green-banded way (left branch). Walk on to take a left turn, where the trail markers now have green and white bands (as seen at the start of the walk). Here there are more sculptures. The track ceases and the trail markers lead you on into a larch plantation. After a few yards you reach a rough grassy ride and, alas, no sign of a marker. Here turn right and after a few more steps along the curving track the trail post comes into view.

Follow the way through dense conifers, winding left and right to reduce the gradient, and continue to a seat. Pause here to enjoy the view. The waymarked path continues down and down and then swings right to pass through a large grassy clearing. Go on along the gently ascending green and white banded track for half a mile. Ignore the forest road that goes off left and in a few steps take the green and white banded footpath that goes off left. Follow this as it descends easily through the pleasing woodland to return you to the car park.

Walk 10

Rusland Valley

Circular walk from Colton Church via Oxen Park and Low Hay Bridge.
Length of walk: 5 miles.
Start/finish: A large open area beside Colton Church. Leave Hawkshead and take the road to Grizedale. Go on through Satterthwaite, Force Mills, Oxen Park and on to the tiny village of Colton, where you turn left. Continue up the narrow lane to take a very sharp left turn that ends at the church.
Terrain: Easy walking. After heavy prolonged rain the path beside Rusland Moss can be under water and a diversion has been included.

This walk takes you through a glorious secret part of High Furness and Rusland. It starts by Colton church, which you might like to visit. Holy Trinity stands on the top of the hill above the hamlet of Colton, from where there is a stunning view. The church is surprisingly large inside and was consecrated in 1578 by Archbishop Sandys. It has a striking west tower. Go through the kissing gate above the church hall. Walk on up the slope and look out for the signposted step-stile through the wall on the left with, beyond, a glorious view of the Coniston range of mountains. Walk ahead, keeping a derelict stone wall to your left and a deciduous wood to the right. Follow the waymark directing you ahead to another stone-stepped stile in the left corner of the pasture. Stride diagonally right towards a waymark set between trees in a row of straggly hawthorns. Walk with the hedge to your right to a post with several arrows on it. Note this point for your return.

Turn half left and walk on to cross a sturdy footbridge over a small stream. Ascend the slope, walking in the same general direction, heading to the right of New Close farm. Beyond the buildings, join an access track and turn left. Take the stone-stepped stile in the wall on your right, just before the first barn on the right. Walk ahead, with the hedge and fence to your left. Pass through a gate and continue uphill, with the wall to your right, to pass through the next gate. Beyond, you can see the rooftops of Oxen Park, towards which you walk. Continue into the small village. Cross the main road and walk right down a narrow lane, between cottages. At the road, cross and turn left. Take the grassy track that leads uphill on the right. Walk on, with a wall to the right, to an idyllic hollow with a beck wandering through and steep bracken-clad slopes coming down almost to the water. Do not ford the beck but go on with the hurrying water to your left. Continue on the clear track to pass through a gate into a walled track. Away to the right is New House, a dwelling that once was the poorhouse for the district. Here the homeless, vagrants and tramps were housed.

Stride on the waymarked way, with a good view of the moor above to your left, to join a delightful track, where you turn left. Walk the lovely way until you reach a gate. Here take the kissing gate on the right and carry on with a wall to your right. Pass through a kissing gate into deciduous woodland and follow the track. Emerge from the trees by a gate and go downhill. Ignore the track that swings away right and press on to a gate into more woodland. Stride on along the grand track to escape the trees by another kissing gate. Ahead stands the gracious Whitestock Hall. Stroll on to join the road, passing through a gate on your

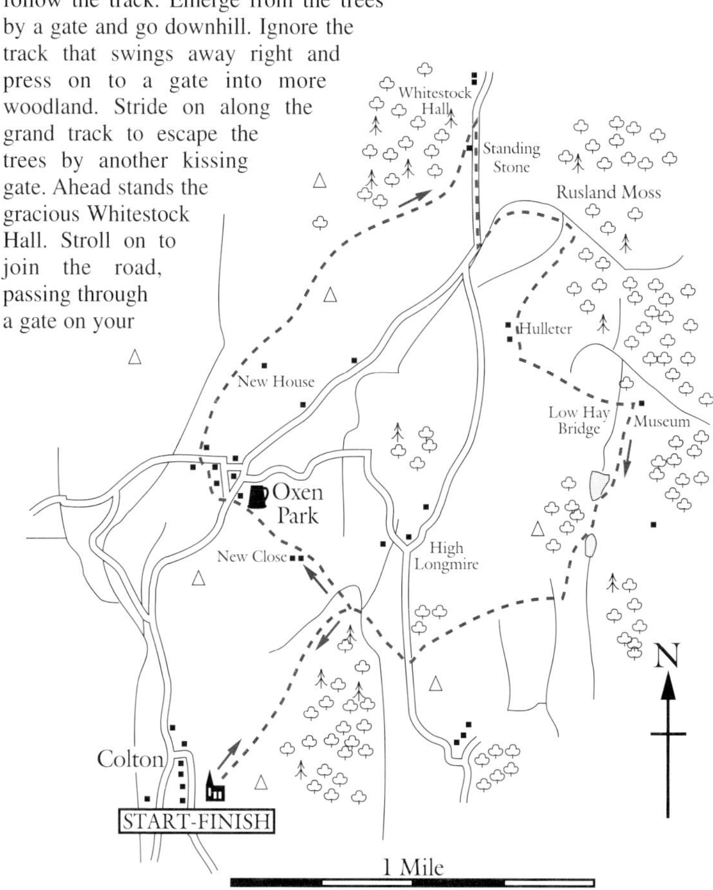

right. Cross the road and stand by the gate to see a standing stone in the middle of the pasture. Turn right and walk with care along the lane for 450 yards. Take the easy-to-miss tiny footbridge set in the hedge on your left that gives access to a signposted track. Turn left, pass through the gate and bear right downhill, keeping to the wall side of the beck. Go ahead to a waymarked stile into the willow and birch woodland of Rusland Moss. In autumn the blackthorn trees along the path are heavy with sloes.

Stroll on along the edge of the wood. (If the way is very wet, move out into the pasture to your right and walk on close to the trees on your left.) The indistinct path through the trees brings you to a footbridge which you cross and a four-armed signpost. Stride across the pasture, at a right angle to the wood, in the direction of Hulleter. Pass through a waymarked gate and then head up towards Hulleter farmhouse, taking a gate to the right of the dwelling. Beyond walk on, bear left and then right through the farm buildings to join a wide signposted track, where you turn left.

Where the track divides, take the left branch and walk down towards the signpost for Low Hay Bridge Nature Reserve. Stay with the wall on the left through two gated pastures and then through a gate into woodland.

Follow the path as it swings right to a signpost that directs you towards Bouth, along a metalled road. To the left of the signpost is a cottage and the museum, which is open only to pre-booked parties and is run by volunteers.

Stroll the pleasing way through the woodland of the reserve. Watch out for the 'toad crossing' sign and the two delectable tarns, one on either side of the road. Cross the cattle grid to leave the wild life sanctuary and walk on. Take the signposted footpath on the right and aim towards the right side of the next waymark post, stationed on a hillock. At the next signpost, ignore the right turn, and walk ahead over a few humps and dips to cross a tractor bridge close to the wall on your left. Go through the gate and stride ahead to follow the wall on your left through two gates to join a narrow lane.

Turn right and in a few yards take the signposted left turn through hazel woodland. Leave the trees by a gate and walk on, following the well waymarked path that descends to a waymarked gate. Beyond walk ahead to the waymark at the end of the straggly hawthorn hedge noted on your outward route. Turn left and stay with the hedge and the wall to the stone-stepped stile to the left of a gate. Beyond walk on with the wall to the right, heading for the wood. Go on with the wood to your left and the derelict wall to the right to another stone-stepped stile in the wall. Beyond follow the wall on the right, downhill to the gate to rejoin your car.